SLEEPING A

Hilary Fannin

Stephen Greenhorn

Abi Morgan

Mark Ravenhill

Methuen Drama is in association with Paines Plough and Salisbury Playhouse

Methuen Drama

First published in the United Kingdom in 1998 by Methuen

3 5 7 9 10 8 6 4 2

This edition published in 1998 by Methuen Drama

A CIP catalogue record for this book is available from the British Library

ISBN 0 413 73270 3

Typeset by MATS, Southend-on-Sea, Essex

SLEEPING AROUND

by

Hilary Fannin
Stephen Greenhorn
Abi Morgan
Mark Ravenhill

First performed at Salisbury Playhouse 11 March 1998
Developed by Paines Plough in association with the
Royal National Theatre Studio

Salisbury Playhouse acknowledges support from Southern Arts, Wiltshire County Council and Salisbury District Council

SALISBURY
PLAYHOUSE

SLEEPING AROUND

TOUR DATES

11 - 21 March
Salisbury Playhouse
01722 320333

23 - 28 March
London, Donmar Warehouse
0171 369 1732

1 - 4 April
Sheffield Crucible Theatre Studio
0114 276 9922

7 - 11 April
Bath, Theatre Royal
01225 448844

21 April
Cardiff, Sherman Arena
01222 230451

23 April
Stamford Arts Centre
01780 763203

25 April
Newbury Corn Exchange
01635 522733

28 April - 2 May
Bristol Old Vic
0117 987 7877

6 May
Crawley, The Hawth Theatre Studio
01293 553636

9 May
Havant, Old Town Hall Arts Centre
01705 472700

13 - 16 May
Mold, Theatr Clwyd
01352 755114

19 - 20 May
Newcastle-upon-Tyne, Live Theatre
0191 232 1232

21 - 23 May
Bolton, Octagon Theatre
01204 520661

26 - 27 May
Scarborough, Stephen Joseph Theatre
01732 370541

28 - 30 May
Derby Playhouse Studio
01332 363275

Paines Plough Theatre Company

Paines Plough plays an important part in the British theatre scene. While only London audiences see many of the new plays being produced, Paines Plough is a truly national company. We tour new plays to small scale theatres the length and breadth of the country.

Paines Plough was founded in 1974 and gives early commissions to numerous talented writers who go on to become well known in theatre, film and television.

Salisbury Playhouse

Salisbury Playhouse presents plays in both its main house and its studio throughout the year and also operates a thriving education department and youth theatre.

The Playhouse has developed its reputation both regionally and increasingly nationally, for a broad ranging and high quality programme of work. Highlights have included the world premiere of Terry Eagleton's new play *Disappearances* and the premiere of *Maddie*, a new musical which transferred to the Lyric, Shaftesbury Avenue in September 1997.

Introduction

Sleeping Around is a glimpse at Britain in the late nineties – a place where people still believe in the potential of a moment's true connection with another human being, in spite of being constantly compartmentalised and brutalised by the many pressures of modern living.

Sleeping Around is a collaboration between four contemporary writers, each carrying their individual voice in a shared form. It is written to be performed by two actors, playing all twelve characters between them.

The kernel of *Sleeping Around* came from an idea by Mark Ravenhill in the offices of Paines Plough. The four writers then began working together during August 1997, when they took part in the first of a series of developmental workshops at the Royal National Theatre Studio. Much research and debate later, *Sleeping Around* draft one emerged. Only one line from that original draft is present in this play.

The process by which we have arrived at this version is a testament to the talent, enthusiasm and vision of the writers and everyone else involved in the piece.

This script was correct at time of going to print.

Characters

Sarah, *single, marketing manager for a major multinational company. Thirty-six.*
Murray, *single, psychology lecturer and academic. Thirty-five.*
Kate, *single, psychology student, part-time job in a toy warehouse. Twenty.*
Joel, *single, electrician, father of Ben aged five. Twenty-five.*
Lyndsey, *lives with Pete. Thirty-one.*
Pete, *lives with Lyndsey. Thirty-four.*
Lorraine, *single, air hostess. Thirty-four.*
Colin, *married to Helen. Thirty-eight.*
Helen, *married to Colin. Thirty-six.*
Greg, *single, computer programmer. Thirty-eight.*
Annie, *single, part-time market researcher. Nineteen.*
Ryan, *single, part-time job in all-night garage. Nineteen.*

Setting

Sleeping Around takes place over one weekend – Friday night to early Monday morning in summer. It is set in a city and the time is present day.

SLEEPING AROUND

by
Hilary Fannin
Stephen Greenhorn
Abi Morgan
Mark Ravenhill

Cast

John Lloyd Fillingham

Sophie Stanton

Director	Vicky Featherstone
Designer	Georgia Sion
Movement Director	Marisa Zanotti
Lighting Designer	Nigel Edwards
Composer	David Benke
Script Development	Jessica Dromgoole
Production Manager	Alison Ritchie
Company Manager	Charlotte Geeves
Stage Manager	Neil Gavin
Stage Management Intern	Louise Dancy (RADA)
Production Photography	Sheila Burnett

With thanks to the National Theatre Studio and to Mel Kenyon at Casarotto Ramsay, Nick Warren, Siamack Salari, Dr. John Goldthorpe, Alison Roberts, Sofia Patel, Kay Hing, Paul Watling, Chris Morley, David Cockrane, Richard Webber, Lucy Hannah, Shaun Dingwall, Angela Clarke, Homes Place Leisure Management, Moët et Chandon, Paul Arditti and Simon King at the sounds department, Royal Court Upstairs.

Paines Plough

Artistic Director	Vicky Featherstone
Administrative Director	Belinda Hamilton
Admin./Marketing Co-ordinator	Lucy Morrison
Literary Director	Mark Ravenhill
Literary Manager	Jessica Dromgoole
Writer-in-Residence	Sarah Kane

Salisbury Playhouse

Artistic Director	Jonathan Church
Executive Director	Rebecca Morland
Marketing Manager	Louise Wright
Marketing Services Manager	Jacqui Byatt
Marketing Assistant	Gavin Brooke
Production Manager	Chris Bagust
Chief Electrician	Peter Hunter
Deputy Chief Electrician	Gina Hills
Assistant Electrician	Ian Burrage
Stage Manager	Brum Gardner
Deputy Stage Managers	Elizabeth Crabtree Cheryl Curley
Assistant Stage Managers	Rhian Thomas Sarah Alford-Smith
Stage Technician	Suresh Chawie
Chief Carpenter	Mike Patch
Deputy Chief Carpenter	Tom Denbury
Scenic Artist	Alexina Smalley
Wardrobe Supervisor	Henrietta Worrall-Thompson
Deputy Wardrobe Supervisor	Penny Peters
Wardrobe Assistants	Harriet Waterhouse Linda Whitlock

HILARY FANNIN (Writer)
Born in Dublin, Ireland and has spent the last fifteen years working as an actress in Irish theatre and television. Her first play *Mackerel Sky* was performed at the Bush Theatre (London) in 1997. *Sleeping Around* is her second outing as a writer. She is currently under commission to the Bush Theatre for a second play.

STEPHEN GREENHORN (Writer)
From West Lothian in Scotland, Stephen has been writing professionally since 1988 and has produced a body of work in Scotland for theatre, film and TV. Visible Fictions have produced two of his plays for children and BBC Radio Four have broadcast three of his radio plays. He wrote *Passing Places* which after its success at the Traverse Theatre in Edinburgh, has received an award from Barclays Stage Partners in collaboration with the Scottish Arts Council to tour in April and May in 1998. He has written episodes for *The Bill* (Carlton TV) and *Where the Heart Is* for United TV's second series which is now in production. He is currently under commission to BBC Films for *Passing Places* and 7:84 Theatre Company.

ABI MORGAN (Writer)
Born in Cardiff, Wales. Her play *Fast Food* (1996/7), which she wrote while on attachment at the National Theatre Studio, was workshopped with the NT company. *On Line* (1995) was one of six plays shortlisted for the Allied Domecq Award at the Bush Theatre. It will be produced at the Nuffield Theatre, Southampton in 1998 (now entitled *Skinned*). Abi is also on attachment to Birmingham Rep. Film / Television: *Gutted* – full length screenplay written as part of the 1996/7 Carlton Screenwriting Course. She is under commission to the BBC and Carlton Television.

MARK RAVENHILL (Writer)
Born in Haywards Heath, England. His first full-length play *Shopping and Fucking* was produced by Out of Joint and the Royal Court Theatre and opened at The Ambassadors Theatre prior to a national tour. It transferred to the West End in June 1997 prior to an international tour. The play has been produced in foreign-language productions in Germany, Holland, Israel, Greece and Scandinavia. It has been optioned for feature film production. His second play *Faust* was produced by ATC (National Tour) in 1997. His earlier work includes *Fist* and *His Mouth* (1995) produced on the London fringe and off-off-Broadway and versions of Wedekind's *Lulu* and Ostrovsky's *Mad Money* for BBC Radio. Mark is currently under commission to Out of Joint and ATC and holds the post of Literary Director at Paines Plough.

VICKY FEATHERSTONE (Director)
Vicky is Artistic Director of Paines Plough. She trained at Manchester University and West Yorkshire Playhouse on the Regional Theatre Young Director Scheme. Vicky's first production for Paines Plough was *Crazyhorse* by Parv Bancil which toured in the Autumn of 1997. She directed *Anna Weiss* for the Traverse Theatre (Edinburgh 1997), which won both Fringe First and Scotland on Sunday's Critics' Awards. Other theatre includes: *Kvetch, Brighton Rock* (West Yorkshire Playhouse), *Two Lips Indifferent Red* (Bush Theatre), *The Glass Menagerie, Christmas Carol, My Mother Said I Never Should* (Bolton Octagon) and *Women Prefer . . .* (Northern Stage). Other work includes: Script Development Executive for United Film and Television Productions, creating *Where The Heart Is* and developing *Touching Evil.*

DAVID BENKE (Composer)
David is a composer/lecturer based in London. His String Quartet *Ungestum* was performed at the

Purcell Room in 1992 and Quintet *319* won first prize in the1992 Royal Overseas League competition for original composition. Music for Primitive Science Theatre Company at the Young Vic/Purcell Room includes *Spell, Imperfect Librarian II, You Have Been Watching . . .* and *Vagabondage*. He wrote the music for *Attempts on Her Life* by Martin Crimp at Royal Court Upstairs in March 1996 and *The Country* by Martin Crimp which was broadcast on BBC Radio Three in November 1997. His operetta for young voices, *Head II Head* was performed by Live Culture at the ENO Works in May 1997. He collaborated with Georgina Starr on *Tuberama*, a multi-media installation at the Ikon Gallery, Birmingham in March 1998.

NIGEL EDWARDS (Lighting Designer)
Most recently, Nigel has designed *Roberto Zucco* and *The Mysteries* for the RSC, *Pleasure,* for Forced Entertainment, and *Bailengangaire* at the Ambassadors for the Royal Court. He also lit Radio One's thirtieth birthday party. He has designed the lights for, and toured extensively with: *Showtime, Speak Bitterness, Hidden J., Club of No Regrets, Emmanuelle, Enchanted, Maina and Lee* (Forced Entertainment); *Hold Me Down, Baldy Hopkins* and *Penny Dreadful* (The Right Size); *Waiting For Godot* (Tottering Bipeds) and for *Louder Than Words, Dreamtime* and *Counting of Years*. He will light *Cleansed* by Sarah Kane at the Royal Court.

JOHN LLOYD FILLINGHAM (Actor)
Trained at Welsh College of Music and Drama. His first appearance was in the world premiere of Jim Cartwright's play *Baths* at the Octagon Theatre Bolton where he has since appeared in *The Importance of Being Earnest, Spring and Port Wine,* and *Waiting for Godot*. Other theatre includes: *I Do* (Royal National Theatre Studio); *The Tempest, The Rise and Fall of Little Voice,* which included a

national tour, and *The Glass Menagerie* (Bristol Old Vic); *The Glory of the Garden* (Duke of Yorks, London); *Road* and *The Doctor's Dilemma* (The Royal Exchange, Manchester). Recently he appeared in *Comedy of Errors* and *The Tempest* (including international tour) at Nottingham Playhouse and *The Atheist's Tragedy* at Birmingham Rep. He played Mozart in *Amadeus* at Chester Gateway and Lysander in *A Midsummer Night's Dream* for the RSC. John played the young F.R. Leavis in *The Last Romantics*, a film for the BBC, and Barnaby Wilde in *Crocodile Shoes* for Red Rooster. Other television work includes an hour-long special of *The Bill* in which he had the guest lead, *September Song* and *Children's Ward* for Granada TV and *Spatz* and *B&B* for Thames. He also played Neil Mitchell in *Coronation Street*. For BBC Radio Three: *Henry I* and *Henry II*, and *School for Scandal*. For BBC Radio Four: *Healthy Pursuits, Cozzy's Last Stand, Letters of Introduction, Looking for Alice, Gabriella and the Gargoyles, Lost Empires* and *A Stone's Throw from the Sea*.

GEORGIA SION (Designer)
From London, Georgia trained on the Motley Theatre Design Course. Theatre work includes: *Afore Night Come* (Theatr Clwyd), *Goldmines* (Clean Break Theatre Company), *The Weavers* (costumes, The Gate Theatre), *Twelfth Night* (Central School of Speech and Drama), *Love on the Dole* (Oldham Coliseum and tour), *Othello* (Watermill Theatre and Tokyo Globe), *The Sunset Ship* (Young Vic Theatre Company, National Gallery), *Shift* (Old Red Lion), *Cut and Running* (BAC), *Richard III* (Arts Threshold) and *Lovers* (RSC Fringe Festival, Stratford). Opera: *A Ronne* (ENO, The Knack), *King and Marshall* (Bloomsbury Theatre), *Four Saints in Three Acts* (Trinity Opera).

SOPHIE STANTON (Actor)
Trained RADA. Theatre includes: *Beautiful Thing* (Bush Theatre & Donmar Warehouse), *Backstroke in a Crowded Pool, Crossing the Equator* (Bush Theatre), *Slaughter City* (RSC, Barbican), *Hindle Wakes, Love's Labours Lost* (Royal Exchange, Manchester), *A Collier's Friday Night* (Hampstead Theatre), *She Stoops To Conquer* (Harrogate) and *Nutcrackers* (Natural Theatre Company). TV includes: *Prime Suspect IV, Shine on Harvey Moon, Dangerous Lady, Dressing for Breakfast, The Sculptress, Birds of a Feather, Get Real, The Peter Principle, The Unknown Soldier, Midsomer Murders, EastEnders, The Mind Machine* and *Girls' Night Out.* Films include: *Shadowlands, Beautiful Thing, Linger* and *Closer.*

MARISA ZANOTTI (Movement Director)
Marisa Zanotti is Artistic Director of Anatomy, receiving commissions from Tramway, CCA and New Moves, Glasgow. Anatomy has shown work nationally and internationally. Marisa's work looks at the body in society and society through the body. She is interested in the tension between dance and other media and the implications for process and form. Marisa directed movement for *Passing Places* (directed by John Tiffany) at the Traverse Theatre, *Dead Elvis* for NVA and *Electra* (directed by Caroline Hall) at the Tramway. She is currently working on a Tramway commission, *Wipe Out.*

Scene One

A city skyline. Night. A corporate balcony. Distant sound of music – a press launch going on, somewhere else.

Sarah *is standing, watching the view, waiting for something. As is* **Murray** *next to her. A logo lights up the moon.*

Murray Wow.

Sarah It wasn't what you were –

Murray No.

Sarah I thought it might be a bit of a –

Murray Surprise.

Sarah Yeah.

Murray Out of this world. (*A beat.*) . . . They'll see this in Manchester?

Sarah They'll see it to Moscow and back.

Murray Satellite links.

Sarah The logo's on a pin-head. A series of digital numbers. All lights, mirrors and fairy dust. If it does the job. It's a big step for us.

Murray A giant leap for mankind. The moon . . . To do that to the moon.

Sarah A capital share until the eve of the millennium, then Pepsi get in.

Murray Quite a coup, lighting up the millennium.

Sarah It was sloppy on our part. They rode on the back of our bid.

Murray Parasites.

Sarah Exactly. (*A beat.*) As long as it reaches the punters.

Sarah *thinks she catches a mocking tone in* **Murray***'s voice. Just resisting touching his mouth.*

You have a little something stuck in your . . .

Murray *picks his teeth.*

Murray Thanks . . . (*Tastes.*) sushi . . .

Sarah Slimy snot on yesterday's take-away. So *passé.* 43 per cent of the 23 to 35 female sector in the metropolitan area had tried sushi by 1997 as opposed to 13 per cent in 1991.

Murray I quite like fish.

Sarah Are you mocking me?

Sarah *laughs flirtatiously.* **Murray** *responds with obviously insincere smile.*

Sarah You've done this before.

Murray Once in a –

Sarah . . . blue moon. You dust down the suit and graze the buffet?

Murray I don't believe in statistics.

Sarah And I'm looking for someone to decode them. (*A beat.*) We're a multinational company. Logo registering works. You don't even know it's us behind half the things you buy. A kid's latest craze, something that beeps and pings and needs you, it will be one of ours. Fuck it, the cure for AIDS and we'll be there. Big business in marketing the elixir of life.

Murray Congratulations. (*A beat.*) What am I doing here?

Sara You're a scientist.

Murray Social scientist.

Sarah *points down to the view below.*

Sarah You know what makes them tick. (*A beat.*) I've read your articles. They're interesting. Very interesting. You're highly respected in your field. We're offering you a lot of money.

Murray It's prostitution.

Sarah It never does a tart harm to know how much she's worth. (*A beat.*) One in three academics believe they're underpaid.

Murray One in three women fear living alone.

Sarah I thought you didn't believe in statistics and anyway where's the link.

Murray There isn't one. That's why I don't believe in statistics.

A beat.

Sarah People are very simple. Shit, eat, sleep.

Murray You want to know why they shit where they shit, why they eat what they eat, why they sleep where they sleep. Work out the recipe.

Sarah We want to diagnose their desires.

Sarah *fondles his tie.*

Murray Create a need.

Sarah All the best things are addictive.

Murray And bad for you.

Sarah *takes the can of coke in her hand and positions it in a place of prominence.*

Murray A cola drink.

Sarah The cola drink.

A beat.

Sarah How old are you?

Murray Thirty-five.

Sarah One in four men lie about their age.

Murray Really.

Sarah *takes the can of coke in her hand.*

Sarah You're not buying it. I've promised the fat cats I can make you.

Sarah *points down below.*

Everyone else is. Her. Him. Everybody. But not you. Not a single eligible male primate in the 23 to 35 year bracket is picking this off the shelf. Why not?

Murray *shrugs.*

Sarah To be frank. We're bigger than tea, we're bigger than coffee –

Murray And you're closing in on water?

Sarah (*a beat*) See. You read my mind. 49 per cent of our share is single women in the 23 to 35 bracket, 22 per cent, tens to teens, 19 per cent, energetic OAPs and that elusive 10 per cent – We really don't know.

Murray It rots your teeth.

Sarah We're talking to the spin doctors. Looking to turn it around. That's where you come in. Your input could be invaluable.

Murray I don't think so.

Sarah The ad teams will be pitching later this week. We want to tap into the wish fulfilment of a generation of men that our figures show we're not reaching, whilst keeping the loyalty of our female consumers.

Sarah *clearly, suggestively stops him.*

Redesign an image that's going to appeal to *him*. That's where the moon fits in. It's powerful, independent, feminine yet asking to be conquered.

Murray The final frontier. Macho rocket-man blasting upwards.

Sarah You've got it. A glistening warrior who fucks space wenches in silver heels –

Murray . . . all day long.

Murray *holds her with his look.*

Sarah It's uncanny how in tune we are.

Murray Spooky.

Sarah Competition is high. They could put a different product up there every night. Internal politics. But if I can get this up there first –

Murray *starts to go.*

Spice, Martini or dreamer?

Murray Thank you for your hospitality –

Sarah It's how you buy. Spice, Martini or dreamer? Do you:

a Know what you want, what you really, really want and get it.
b Don't care what it is or where you buy it. Any time, any place, anywhere. Or:
c Want it but know how much it will cost you and so go for the shop brand instead.

Murray Christ, a fuck-up.

Sarah Maybe it takes one to know one.

Murray Maybe I don't fit into a category.

Sarah Everybody does.

Murray Maybe I'd rather make up my own.

Sarah I bet I could tell you what you buy. If you bothered to use your store reward card I could even check this off against your receipt.

Murray But I don't.

Sarah Bachelors in their mid-thirties don't seem to.

Murray I could be married.

Sarah You're not.

A beat.

I have six months to make this work.

Murray Or . . . What can they do to you?

Sarah They lit up the moon. They can do anything they want.

Murray Your neck's on the line.

He leans over and smells her perfume.

Murray (*sniffing*) Expensive.

Sarah Contradiction. Calvin Klein.

Murray You change every six months when that graduate in the fast track starts smelling the same.

Sarah Late-night shopper. Pork pie, Guinness. Loo freshener when she's around.

Murray You look in the mirror every morning and see your mother.

Sarah Wine club. One foreign holiday a year. Private pension.

Murray You wonder if anyone will ever pick you off the shelf?

A beat.

Sarah Everyone has their sell-by date.

Sarah *undoes his flies, slips her hand in and slowly starts to masturbate him.*

Murray *gazes at the logo on the moon.*

Murray It's a trick. A gimmick. People see that and they don't feel so alone. It's them and it. Smiling down at them from the moon. Primitive. Creating desire only utterly unavailable. Who can ever reach the moon? The great punchline is they can. Because it's in every superstore. The joke's on us. ICU. I think you've got a . . . a . . . a . . . winner!

He comes. **Sarah** *takes her hand away and zips his flies.*

Sarah You'll take the job.

Murray *kisses her.*

Murray You live alone don't you Sarah?

A beat.

Sarah You'll take the job.

Murray I don't think so.

As he goes.

23 to 35 year old men? Shoplifters.

Sarah *is left standing alone. Fireworks and party in the distance –*

A silent buzz of light flicker as the logo breaks down.

Sarah Oh fuck.

Scene Two

A houseboat, glass bottomed, cramped. Light from floor. **Kate** *is hunkered down, watching the river through the floor.* **Murray** *sits behind her in a chair – dispassionate.*

Murray What do you see?

Kate Nothing.

Murray River fish are universally bleak.

Kate Oh.

Murray They're lucky.

Kate Why?

Murray Why? Because unlike their more ostentatious tropical counterparts, they don't end up decorating the suburban garden. Are you cold?

Kate Yes.

Pause.

I wasn't sure if I'd find you in, I just took a chance that . . . (*Starting.*) Oh god! It's an eel.

Murray Purveyors of repulsion. Did it frighten you?

Kate I thought . . . No.

Murray Good.

He smiles.

Kate Good.

She smiles. Pause

Murray Why did you come here?

Kate You. You . . . Why here? Why a boat?

Murray Water, protects my freedom.

Beat.

Kate You know me.

Murray I do?

Kate I was at your lecture today.

Murray/Kate Love Myself, Feed Myself.

Kate I have all your books. Third row up on the left; I sat next to the girl with the harelip. Next to her, I looked desirable, better choice. It's all here in your book.

Murray That's alright. I remember.

Kate You said today, it's all about consumption. Our desire to consume. To be subsumed.

Murray I didn't say that.

Kate I know exactly what you mean. We need to be the closest you can get, the absolute dead pit centre. To exist inside someone. To be consumed by someone. Two halves, as you said . . .

Murray I never . . .

Kate . . . make one complete. I understand you. My mother . . . I was a twin . . . you know, inside her. There were two of us inside my mother. And then one day my sister just fell out, splat, on the supermarket floor. This little embryonic naked rat. Pink like those prawns they cover in mayonnaise so you can swallow them. You never think that even digested you're not safe.

Murray You were . . . ?

Kate A twin, yes. For a time.

Murray And then your sister . . . ?

Kate Abseiled from the womb at twenty-two weeks. Dropped . . .

Murray . . . On the supermarket floor?

Kate Yes.

Murray Christ.

Pause.

And what did you do?

Kate Hung on, stretched –

Murray It's late. I have had a tedious evening and, entertaining as your pre-natal tales are, I'm going to ask you to leave.

Kate Psychology is my favourite subject.

Murray I'm so glad.

Kate *produces a fun-pack of Twixes.*

Go . . . What are you doing?

Kate Exactly what you said. I'm loving myself. I'm feeding myself. Cheers.

Murray Cheers?

Kate To digestion. You should be saying congratulations.

Murray Why?

Kate Family-pack. The other twenty-four have been in my stomach for hours.

Murray Why –

Kate I usually stick a Biro down my throat.

Murray I don't even know you.

Kate My mouth is an intersection. Two-way traffic meets at my teeth . . .

Murray Please.

Kate . . . like casualties pulled from the wreckage.

Murray Shut up.

Kate Shut up.

Beat.

I wish you'd eat me.

Murray Face the wall.

Kate What?

Murray I can't bear to look at your mouth. Face the wall.

Kate I want you to . . .

Murray You trust me don't you? You believe in me?

Kate I want you to help me stay alive.

Murray Lie down.

Murray *pushes* **Kate** *face down on the floor of the boat.*

What do you see?

Kate I don't

Murray Brown trout, carp, eel . . .

Murray *turns her around to face him.*

Do you know what the helpless inspire?

Kate Protection?

Murray Loathing.

He turns her back to the floor and begins to fuck her unexcitedly.

Those brown fish bore me rigid. There is not a day goes past when I don't think about their oceanic sisters, yellow-finned, crimson-bellied delicacies in a turquoise sea.

Kate But you're here.

Murray Yes.

Kate To help me.

Murray Yes.

Scene Three

A warehouse. **Kate** *carries in a very large cardboard box.* **Joel** *stands watching her.*

Joel I'm not a convict.

Kate Right.

Joel I'm not just out of prison. Which is what most people think.

Kate Really?

Joel Oh, yes. Most people look at you and they think 'security guard, must have just got out of prison'. Did you think that?

Kate No, no.

Joel Don't be embarrassed. Everybody assumes . . . It's just a way of paying the bills, y'know. Started today. And you . . . you look like an educated person.

Kate Really?

Joel Oh yeah. There are people who do things and people

who have things done to them. And you're a doer. You've been educated. I'm right aren't I?

Kate Well, yes.

Joel So – this is your gap year.

Kate Not exactly.

Joel Have I got the right word? So, you're saving, yes? – For what? India probably. Bathe in the Ganges. Paint bits of your body with – what's the? Like the shampoo . . .

Kate Henna.

Joel Henna, exactly . . . Henna. You're about to embark on an adventure.

Kate I work in a warehouse.

Joel Well, now yes. For now. Do you ever go to bed?

Kate Yes.

Joel Because if you're here all night . . .

Kate My agency send me on a casual basis.

Joel When there's a rush on?

Kate Exactly.

Joel And now there's a rush on?

Kate And now there's a rush on. Excuse me I have to . . .

Kate *starts to open the box.*

Joel And you want me to fuck off?

Kate Yeah. Fuck off.

Joel See, that's what I like about the educated. You've got broader minds than the rest of us. You don't mind the occasional fuck.

Kate Well . . .

Joel Saying fuck occasionally.

Kate Please look I have to . . .

Joel And when you get home to the boyfriend, another educated person, it's all 'How was your fucking day?', 'fucking terrible', 'oh how fucking awful', 'Yes, there was this fucking boring guy, all through the night talking away and no fucking education'.

Kate No, no.

Joel Why is there a rush on?

Kate I don't know. I just take things out of boxes. I rip open cardboard boxes and try to avoid the staples. Huge staples that often rip my hands. See?

Joel Go on. Tell me. Why is there a rush on?

Kate Then I put the goods in a big trolley. Then I fold, I squash the cardboard boxes until they're flat. And I feed them into an incinerator which burns them.

Joel What goods? You must know.

Kate Then I wheel the goods out on to the shop floor and load them on to the shelves. Then it's back to the beginning. I don't ask questions.

Joel I want to know. Tell me. Why is there a rush on?

Kate Ripping open the cardboard boxes and tying to avoid the staples.

Joel I don't want to fuck off and not know why there's a rush on.

Beat.

I'm not gonna fuck off.

Beat.

Kate It's a Japanese . . . it's a gadget thing. Little electronic box thing for kids. But it's needy.

Joel Yeah?

Kate It's a twin, cyber-twin. Takes the kid's face and programmes it in so it's got the kid's face looking up at the kid. Copies the kid's voice. Calls out in the kid's voice when it needs the kid. 'I want you to help me stay alive'. The kid pushes buttons. Feed it, let it sleep, wake it up. Nurture it. 'You make me feel safe'. Because if you don't nurture your cyber-twin . . .

Joel It dies.

Kate (*laughs*) Yeah, it dies. Some chip somewhere switches off and then . . . (*Laughs.*) . . . you have to buy another one. You have to buy this expensive piece of tat again. And again and again.

Joel But if it means that much to the child . . .

Kate It's disgusting. It disgusts me. And to make money like that. Torture a kid like that. Looking after a gadget when there are people to look after. (*Laughs.*) Poor fuckers.

Joel Yes but if a child . . . if you had a child.

Kate I don't want a child.

Joel But if you had a child and that child couldn't sleep, if that child called out to you in the middle of the night because it didn't have . . .

Kate Then I'd tell it to get a life. Or I'd give it away.

Joel You wouldn't.

Kate I would.

Silence. **Kate** *turns back to the box.*

Joel I've got a son.

Silence.

My son is being looked after by a baby-sitter. A reliable person with a degree.

Silence.

Give me one.

Kate Sorry?

Joel One of them Japanese things. Give me one.

Kate I've got to account for them. I can't . . .

Joel His mum's got him one. I know. We speak once a week. On a Thursday evening. On the telephone. And she told me – not in a loaded way – in a neutral way – she told me that she'd got hold of one. Friend of a friend. And when he goes over there, when she gets the boy on Saturday, she's going to give him . . . and he'll love it. He'll love her. Who do you love the most? Mummy, I love Mummy the most. So if I can . . . I thought if I got in as a security guard then I could find a way . . . You see? You see?

Kate It's not healthy.

Joel I need him. I want him to love me.

Kate On my course we'd call that dysfunctional.

Joel Yes, yes it's . . . but I can't bear it if . . . my heart will break. I'm begging you . . .

Kate Begging me?

Joel Begging you.

Kate *takes a cyber-twin out of the box and holds it above her head.*

Kate Show me.

Joel You . . .

Kate Illustrate. Embody . . . begging.

Joel *kneels.*

That's it. That's it.

Kate *hits him hard across the face.*

And now . . .

Kate *pulls up her skirt.*

Persuade.

Kate *pushes his head into her groin.*

Who do you love? Who do you love the most?

Scene Four

Dawn. A kitchen. The only light, first rays of dawn through a blind. **Joel**, *just in and still rough from the night before, stands, a box of Coco Pops in his hand.* **Lyndsey**, *jogging pants and a pint of milk, stands nervously by the door. An awkward pause.* **Joel** *flicks the light. Nothing.*

Joel Crap.

Lyndsey *laughs, a nervous reaction.*

Lyndsey What do you –

Joel Electrician. And I can't even change a light bulb.

They laugh.

Lyndsey.

Lyndsey Yeah. (*A beat.*) Joel.

Joel Same one.

More nervous laughter; a long pause.

Why don't you sit down?

Lyndsey I went to buy some milk.

Joel Yeah. Coco Pops –

Lyndsey Yeah.

Joel . . . are good with milk.

Lyndsey . . . Sorry . . . Here have (*Handing over the milk.*) . . . I couldn't sleep. It was really for the air as much as anything . . .

Joel (*holding up the Coco Pops box*) Can't get him up without them.

Lyndsey You've got a . . .

Joel Four nearly five.

Lyndsey You don't look old enough to . . .

Joel I'm not . . . Hopeless at it. Fatherhood. (*A beat.*) Sit down. I'll open the fridge . . . door . . . It's not a bad . . . I mean it does give . . .

Joel *eagerly opens the fridge door, which offers a shaft of light.*

. . . some kind of light . . .

A long beat.

Lyndsey You live –

Joel Just me and the boy . . . I shouldn't really leave him but . . .

Lyndsey You've been – Your clothes look like you've been –

Joel On a bit of a mission.

Lyndsey Yeah?

Joel Yeah . . .

Lyndsey Impossible . . . Mission impossible?

Joel Mission accomplished.

Lyndsey I won't ask.

Joel Don't – You want some –

Lyndsey No, I'll go now. . .

Joel *roots through the fridge. Nothing except –*

Joel Breakfast I could do you some –

Sniffing a half open tin –

Shit on toast.

Lyndsey *laughs nervously.*

Sit down.

Lyndsey I'm fine.

Joel You sure?

Lyndsey Fine.

Joel Only you weren't exactly . . .

Lyndsey Jogging . . . I'd stopped for a rest. I didn't really fancy it. Garages. Only place that never closes. Twenty-four hours, 365 days a year.

Joel (*a beat*) It will have to be Coco Pops. I've normally finished the box before he's up anyway. Ben. His name's Ben.

Lyndsey That's nice.

Joel You got any?

Lyndsey *shakes her head.* **Joel** *lays them out two bowls, opening up the Coco Pops and pours them in.*

Lyndsey I'm alright . . .

Joel It's no problem . . . You're alright.

He hands a bowl to **Lyndsey**. *She reluctantly takes them. She pours the milk.*

A long pause.

No table. I keep meaning to get one but – Sit down . . .

They sit and eat.

I haven't been moved in long.

Lyndsey No. (*A beat.*) How long?

Joel Only about three –

Lyndsey Three months is nothing. No wonder you –

Joel . . . years.

Lyndsey Oh –

A long pause as they eat in silence.

Joel You live near . . . the garage.

Lyndsey Not far . . .

Joel Go there a lot do you . . . ?

Lyndsey No . . . sort of . . . sometimes . . . lately . . .

Joel When you can't sleep?

Lyndsey I'm just not . . . at the moment . . .

A pause.

I don't even know you.

Joel You're alright. He's upstairs. I've got a kid upstairs.

Lyndsey *holds his look for a moment.*

You're alright.

Lyndsey I think he thought I was a bit of a nut. The lad at the garage. You can't get in. The shop part. At night. They lock them in. It's all timed. And I wanted some milk and he wouldn't open the door. I had to point to what I wanted and then –

Joel He passes it through the hatch.

Lyndsey He passes it through the hatch. Only I freaked a bit at the door. You saw.

Joel Yeah.

Lyndsey You were watching me.

Joel Yeah. I mean . . . Only . . . Because I was waiting and he couldn't serve until . . . You were . . .

Lyndsey You know when you're pushing and you should be pulling. He kept on gesturing to me and this booming voice comes over the Tannoy. 'Stand back from the door. This is alarm timed. Do not initiate an entry.' Only the weird thing is he's not moving his lips. He's looking at me like a gorm and then, you know, I'm not really awake and it's like the God of the Garage talking from above. And I'm thinking how does he do that? Throw his voice like that? I only came out for a pint of milk and now I've got the God of the Garage –

A long pause.

I am a nut. I can hear myself . . . I'd think I was a nut.

Joel *shakes his head.*

Joel You look alright to me.

Lyndsey It's a three o'clock. (*Checking her watch.*) Four o'clock in the morning thing.

They carry on eating in silence.

Joel Three second memories. You have to have . . . To work in those places. It's so when they've worked their way around the travel sweets and chamois leathers they forget why they are there and so it gives them something to do all over again. Keeps them occupied. It's all part of the training.

Lyndsey *laughs.*

I know. I got fired from one once. Four second brain. Hopeless if you've got that extra second. You remember in that idle extra sixty nano of a second . . . When you're twiddling your thumbs and picking your . . . This is it for the whole night and then. Bingo relief – you forget again. But it's very distracting. You do . . . I did . . . I would . . . I mean you do . . . nick all the sweets and dismantle the travel nail-kits to pass the time.

A beat.

They noticed.

Lyndsey I should . . . I'm keeping you up.

Joel No. I probably won't go to bed anyway now. Have some tea? Just . . . I haven't asked you . . . A cup of tea?

Lyndsey No . . .

Joel Have some more?

Joel *pours her some more Coco Pops.*

Lyndsey I don't. . .

Joel We've got the whole box to get through yet.

Lyndsey I don't . . .

Joel Go on . . .

Lyndsey *takes the milk off him and pours.*

Lyndsey It must have been a heavy night.

Joel (*gesturing to her top*) You've still got your nightie on . . .

Lyndsey Yes . . . Look I don't . . . I wanted some fresh air . . . I walked for a while around the common. We've got a house on the common. We. Joel . . . I'd . . .

Joel I'm not stopping you . . . Do you think? . . . I just thought . . . You looked like you needed to –

Lyndsey I did . . . I mean . . . You looked at me . . . And I needed to . . . talk to . . .

Joel Stay . . .

Lyndsey I don't know you.

Joel You do now . . . I introduced myself . . . Stay and then you can go when you want to . . .

Lyndsey *sits back down.*

Joel (*pulling out a plastic toy from Coco Pops*) Last dinosaur for my collection. (*A beat.*) There's nothing to be frightened of.

Lyndsey I just suddenly couldn't be bothered. To jog . . . to do . . .

Joel Yeah. Eat this right thing, do that right thing, be this right thing . . .

Lyndsey I think that's important. I think health is important. Spiritual health is important.

Joel Yeah . . . Right . . .

Lyndsey Visualization, meditation. Normally I do things to help me sleep.

Joel Yeah right . . .

Lyndsey But this time . . .

Joel Bed's too big . . . ?

Lyndsey Bed's too big . . . It's a three o'clock . . .

Joel Four o'clock . . .

Lyndsey It was three o'clock then . . . Three o'clock in the morning thing . . .

Joel That's why you got to get yourself a kid . . .There's always the top bunk if you can't sleep . . . It's always . . . 'Dad are you pissed again?' 'No someone's just nicked the door to me room.' Always gets him. Someone to talk to.

Lyndsey You drink?

Joel Not enough. Are you hot in that? Take your jacket off if you want.

Lyndsey *shakes her head.*

So the bed's too big . . .

Lyndsey *looks at him.*

So the bed's too big.

Lyndsey I am frightened . . .

Joel Don't be . . . So the bed's too big . . .

Lyndsey And your mind is always racing and so I think I'll go jogging . . .

Joel It's dangerous . . .

Lyndsey It's more dangerous to stay inside sometimes . . .

Joel This time of night. You could of . . . Lucky I . . .

Lyndsey Met you . . . ?

Joel I found you . . .

Lyndsey It's that feeling when you wake up and you're so alone and so you distract your mind. You think . . . Overdraft and dying your tea towels and this room is shite and you start seeing cellulite on your wrists. You find cellulite on your wrists at three o'clock in the morning. Anything to take your mind away from what is really going on. What you really feel, what you really truly feel is so . . . Just you on the planet. And then I see him . . . Petrol pump boy in his tank . . .

A long pause.

Joel Are you still frightened?

Lyndsey *nods.*

Get yourself a kid . . . I love the smell of his breath . . . I lie on the top bunk. Listening . . . Sobers me up . . . Reminds me to clear the empties and fag ash out before he gets up . . . You should get yourself one of them . . .

Lyndsey Joel . . .

Joel Lyndsey . . .

Joel *leans forward and wipes a dribble of milk that has spilt down her chin and neck, pausing on her neck.*

You're dripping Coco Pops.

Lyndsey I was thirsty . . . I wanted some milk . . . Can you understand that?

Joel Yeah . . .

Lyndsey At home I go to the fridge. I want cow's milk. I want cold cow's milk. And I want to talk to someone. I don't care what but I want to hear someone talk to me. To want to talk to me. It's a simple transaction. I don't want to talk through a piece of Perspex. I want to be able to touch him. I don't want to have to beg for it . . .

Joel Lyndsey.

Lyndsey I didn't come looking for . . . I didn't come . . .

Joel I know. (*A beat.*) It's not wrong. To want someone. It's not wrong to want to just be with someone . . .

Lyndsey I don't want you to get the wrong idea . . . I don't want . . .

Joel We could just lie together . . .

Lyndsey I just feel . . .

Joel You could listen to me. Just listen to my breath . . . I'm too tired to be honest but you could just be with me.

Lyndsey You see I keep tapping on the Perspex and he says, 'Listen . . . I can't let you in . . . It's on a timer . . . It won't let out till the next shift . . .' I say . . . 'That's dangerous . . . That's really very dangerous . . .' He looks at me . . . like I'm the one in the tank . . . 'It senses fire and I've an emergency number in case of accidents.' He's only maybe twenty. And I say 'I don't mean that . . .' I say . . . 'I don't mean that . . .'

A long beat. **Joel** *gets up.*

Joel Have some toast.

Lyndsey *nods her head in agreement.*

Lyndsey Joel. (*A beat.*) And we could just lie together.

Joel Yeah, Lyndsey . . . And we could just lie together.

Lyndsey *eats her cereal.* **Joel** *makes toast. The sun comes up. The bleep of a cyber-twin.* **Joel** *ignores it.* **Lyndsey** *searches for the noise.*

Scene Five

A park. Daytime.

Lyndsey And now there's a garden. Come into the garden. Step into the garden. That's it. You're in the garden. And take time, take a moment to look around the garden.

Pause.

And smell the garden. Breathe in the . . . flowers, herbs, the . . . the grass is wet, the smell of wet grass. Breathe it in, deep breaths. Yes. One . . . two . . . three. Deep breaths.

Pause.

Yes. That's it. And now a gate.

Pause.

And the gate opens and there's light and it's shining and it's bright and it's warm and flows into your body and you feel the light and the light is healing you. The light is flowing through your body. Yes, good. Breathe in the healing, breathe it in.

Pause.

And now – oh look – there's a path ahead of you. And the path is your future. And it's shining, it's . . . imbued with the light. There are no obstacles . . . nothing to block the path and you step on to the path, into the future with no fear, you fear nothing.

Pause.

Now then. I'm going to count down from five and when you're ready you will open your eyes and you'll wake up refreshed and calm. Five . . . four . . . three . . . two . . . one.

Pause.

Yes?

Pete Yes. Thank you.

They kiss.

Thank you.

Lyndsey Did you see it?

Pete Oh yes.

Lyndsey You saw everything?

Pete Oh yes. Clear as anything. Clear as you are now. Yes.

Lyndsey Because there are other ones. If you want to try another one.

Pete No. That's fine.

Lyndsey Everyone will have slightly different . . . triggers.

Pete No. Garden, path, light. Perfect.

Lyndsey There's all sorts of scenarios.

Pete You tried it yourself?

Lyndsey We tried them on each other. That was all part of the course. Before we went out there, out here and tried them on real people . . . on people out here, we had to try them on each other.

Pete And what did it do for you?

Lyndsey I don't . . .

Pete Garden-path-light. Did it do it for you? Beaches, sun? Forests, summer rain? Cornfields?

Lyndsey No.

Pete No?

Pause.

Lyndsey I couldn't . . . I didn't see anything. There was . . . I was blocked. I was frightened and it made me blocked and I couldn't see anything.

Pete Just . . . ?

Lyndsey Nothing. Blank. Void. But I'm . . . look . . . I'm working on it.

Pete Sure.

Lyndsey Because look I do believe, I do fundamentally believe that you'll live. You have a future and it's healthy and long and . . .

Pete Sure.

Lyndsey It's just when I get frightened . . .

Pete Of course.

They cuddle.

Lyndsey This is nice. Holding you is nice.

Pete It's very nice.

They carry on cuddling until **Lyndsey** *rubs against* **Pete** *in a sexual way.*

No.

Lyndsey No?

Pete I don't want you to . . . not like that.

Lyndsey Okay.

Pause.

I was just showing you . . .

Pete I know.

Lyndsey I've still got the same feelings . . .

Pete Sure.

Lyndsey I still want you.

Pete You want a shag?

Lyndsey I love you. I want you.

Pete You want a shag?

Lyndsey I want a shag. That's not the word I'd . . .

Pete I don't want a shag.

Lyndsey Ever?

Pete I don't . . . probably. Ever.

Lyndsey Is that the medication? Western medicine. All those chemicals, toxic, and they change, it's poisoning you.

Pete Doctor says it's significantly prolonging my life.

Lyndsey Of course.

Pete Poisoning me and significantly prolonging my life?

Lyndsey You'll live longer than me.

Pete Don't think so.

Lyndsey These new drugs, this breakthrough . . .

Pete We'll see.

Lyndsey And you're going to live until . . . ninety and never . . . never have a sexual relationship?

Pete That's right.

Lyndsey Are you frightened of your body?

Pete No.

Lyndsey Are you scared that you're not attractive?

Pete No.

Lyndsey You just don't want me.

Pause.

I've done everything I can. I've read everything. All that stuff you wouldn't look at. Medical books and trials and treatment reports. I could probably qualify as a doctor, stuff I've read. So that we can understand what's happening to you. And then the other stuff. The herbalists, the healers . . . appointments I've made and then you tell me you're too fatigued to go. The weekend courses. So I can give you massage and aromatherapy, affirmation, visualisation, t'ai chi. What else can I do? Tell me if there's anything else I can do to show you that I love you, how much I love you?

Pete I didn't see anything.

Lyndsey You . . . ?

Pete I didn't see any of it. The garden, the gate, the path. They weren't there.

Lyndsey No?

Pete All that stuff. That rubbish. I did it for you.

Lyndsey You saw a void?

Pete No.

Lyndsey What did you see?

Pete Doesn't matter.

Lyndsey What did you see?

Pete I saw you. I saw you and your need. Your need that says 'Love me. I want to be loved. And you're dying because you don't really love me. If you really loved me you wouldn't die.'

Beat.

That's what I saw.

Lyndsey I see.

Beat.

I see.

Beat.

Well fuck you. Fuck you. Fuck off then. Yeah and crawl under a stone and give up and be selfish and die if you want to. Because if that's what you fucking want then I'm not going to fucking stop you.

Pause.

Pete I love you.

Pause.

Lyndsey I still want you. I still want you to fuck me. Nothing's changed.

Pete Nothing?

Lyndsey Nothing.

Pete I have eight lesions. Three are on my upper body. Four on my lower body. The biggest one is on my right foot and has a circumference of several inches. And one – a smallish one – is on my groin directly above my penis.

Lyndsey I don't see them.

Pete Of course you see them.

Lyndsey They don't mean anything to me. Because I love you.

Pete Because you want to be loved. And you want to be loved so badly that you'll even allow a leper, a disfigured, suppurating leper fuck you so for that moment, just for a moment you could feel that you were loved.

Lyndsey You mustn't think of yourself . . . if your self-image is so negative . . .

Pete And your self-image, your esteem must be so low, it must be non-existent.

Lyndsey You hate yourself.

Pete You hate yourself.

Lyndsey I love you.

Pete I love you.

Lyndsey Then fuck me.

Pete I can't.

Lyndsey You won't.

Pause.

Pete It doesn't all have to be one person, you know?

Lyndsey Mmmm?

Pete Looking after. Being with. Worrying about. Fucking. You don't have to do them all with the same person.

Pause.

Do the fucking with someone else.

Lyndsey I don't want that.

Pete Just the fucking. (*Smiles.*) Do any of the other stuff and I'll chop your tits off.

Lyndsey That's not what I want.

Pete I'm giving you permission. Go forth and copulate.

Lyndsey No.

Pete Plenty of healthy dick out there.

Lyndsey I don't want it. I couldn't do it.

Pete You've never thought about it?

Lyndsey No. Never.

Pete Never been tempted?

Lyndsey Never.

Pete It's never for a moment crossed your mind?

Lyndsey It's never crossed my mind.

Pete So. If I was a . . . a paraplegic, you'd still want to shag me and nobody else?

Lyndsey Yes.

Pete I'm a stump. I've no arms and no legs. What do you do?

Lyndsey I'd fuck you. As long as I could look at you, look into your eyes and tell you I loved you as we came.

Pete (*smiles*) Sick bitch.

Lyndsey (*smiles*) Sick bitch in love.

Pete (*smiles*) Sick bitch in love . . . with the hots.

Pause.

Lie back.

Lyndsey Yeah?

Pete Lie back and close your eyes.

She lies back and closes her eyes. Her legs are together.

You're in a garden. And it's morning and it's been raining or maybe just a dew, a heavy dew. But there's a smell, the smell of grass that's been cut the day before. Fresh and sweet and refreshing. And you roll in the grass until you're wet. Until your clothes are wet. Until your nipples are erect and they stand out from your wet blouse. And now I'm there and I'm wet too. You can see my body through my clothes. And I'm looking at you. I'm taking in your body.

Gently he eases open her legs.

And you feel that you want me. And I feel that I want you. And we both know that we feel the same way and we know what we want to do and we don't want to do it too fast because this moment is too perfect but we know we have to do it.

He gently slides his hands inside her knickers and starts to masturbate her.

And we move together and I unbutton you slowly and you unbutton me. And my tongue . . . where is my tongue?

Lyndsey Ear . . . neck . . . breast . . . nipple . . . breast . . . neck . . . ear.

Pete And my chest. There are lesions.

Lyndsey No. This is before.

Pete And there are lesions.

Lyndsey And I kiss the lesions. And I take your nipple and I caress it with my tongue. A little bite.

Pete Yes. And we feel the same thrill in our bodies and now a switch has been switched and every touch, every breath . . . vibrates. And now . . .

Lyndsey Your cock.

Pete Yes. You take my cock. You hold my cock and you work my cock as I work your cunt.

Lyndsey I'm ready.

Pete And you roll a condom . . .

Lyndsey No.

Pete There's a condom.

Lyndsey I don't want . . .

Pete There's always a condom.

Lyndsey It's just a story. There's no condom.

Pete There's a condom. And I'm inside you and we move together, we hold on to each other and we look into each other's eyes.

Lyndsey I love you.

Pete I love you.

She starts to come.

That's it. Oh yes that's it. Don't love me when I'm dead. Find someone else when I'm dead and love them and fuck them and come with them.

Her orgasm is reaching climax.

But love me for now. Love me until I die. Yes, that's it. Good. Good.

Scene Six

An indoor swimming-pool. **Pete** *and* **Lorraine** *loll.*

Lorraine *hums with earphones on.* **Pete** *watching her.* **Lorraine** *removes earphones. Looks at him.*

Lorraine You know, some people pray for stigmata. It was a dreadful realisation.

Pete What was?

Lorraine That I would never present a Eurovision. I love a smattering of multilingual. I can say 'Good Morning' in thirty-seven languages. And 'Fuck me, I'm a doctor' in Portuguese.

Pete Would you, if I was?

Lorraine If you were?

Pete A doctor. Would you fuck me?

Lorraine Do you really think they do it? I always assumed they dismantled themselves and got into a drawer. (*Beat.*) Yes.

Pete Yes?

Lorraine I would fuck you. If you were a doctor.

Pete Thank you.

Pause.

Lorraine Do you know many?

Pete Doctors? (*Beat.*) Not as well as they know me.

Lorraine *has a long look at* **Pete**.

Don't look at me.

Lorraine How ill *are* you?

Pete Very.

Long beat.

Lorraine *sings from an upbeat Irish Eurovision-winning song.*

Beat. He touches his chest.

Pete Thank you.

Lorraine For?

Pete Accepting my invitation to float.

Lorraine That's alright. I'm used to dealing with unusual requests.

Pete You're . . . ?

Lorraine An air hostess.

Pete Oh right . . . right.

Lorraine Stop overs. I stop over. Lobbies.

Pete Yes?

Lorraine I like them. And hairdressing salons and dark bars and tarmacadam and acrylic fingernails. These are a . . . (*Looks at the sky.*) Do you know it's seven p.m. in New York City. They'll be expecting a moon.

Pause.

Pete I like . . .

Lorraine Yes?

Pete Air hostesses in lobbies. Long legs in dark bars. Your limbs in chlorine.

Beat.

Lorraine You come here . . . ?

Pete . . . often. To float.

Lorraine I'm . . .

Pete . . . stopping over.

Lorraine . . . stopping over, yes. (*Lying back.*) This makes a change. I usually drown in a bottle of blue label and a co-pilot. Are you married?

Pete No.

Lorraine How did you get it?

Pete How did . . . ?

Lorraine Your lesions. The hallmark of your disease. How did you get it?

Pete I asked you not to look at me.

Lorraine You asked me to swim with you. You plucked me from a dark bar. You chose me as your witness. How did you get your disease?

Pete (*beat*) I was fucked by a man on a balcony.

Lorraine You too?

Pete Simple gratification. The desire to be fucked without allegiance. (*Beat.*) The kissing and carving . . .

Lorraine The kissing and carving?

Pete A lifetime of mothers, brothers, ball sports and partaking and kissing and carving.

Lorraine And then you got fucked on a balcony?

Pete It was somebody's birthday. I also got fucked under trees and once in a pigeon loft.

Lorraine *laughs.*

Did you ever do it on your aeroplane?

Lorraine Fuck the aeroplane. I did it on the baggage carousel. (*Beat.*) Tell me . . .

Pete Tell you?

Lorraine About the first time.

Pete The first time?

Lorraine Ever.

Pete The first time ever was with a woman. It was hysterical – she must have been forty. I was fifteen.

Lorraine Liar.

Pete Alright – seventeen. She told me I looked like Ringo. Said her sister had slept with Paul McCartney, said that music ran in her family, and warts. Had Angie Dickinson's autograph Sellotaped to the bedroom mirror and a parade of laminated kittens on her wall.

Lorraine How was the sex?

Pete Fantastic. Very sentimental.

Beat.

Lorraine How old are you?

Pete Thirty-five.

Lorraine Don't one in five men lie about their age?

Pete Thirty-five years, eight months and twenty-seven days, slipping under the wire to thirty-five years, eight months and twenty-eight days. I hoard my age, reckon it. Each day clocked, my tiny act of subversion.

Lorraine What's the terror?

Pete That I will die and reconstitute and spin around limbo in my mother's laundry basket. Eternity, I suppose, is the greatest terror. Conscious eternity.

Pause.

(*Shaking his head*.) You?

Lorraine Me?

Pete The first time.

Lorraine I don't remember.

Pause.

Pete Kiss me.

Lorraine I don't kiss. Can't. My mouth is too full. Alphabets of information roaming around my teeth. Oxygen. Emergency. Whistle. Strip-lighting. I keep my mouth clear of hand baggage, but I get up on anything with a pulse.

Pete No.

Lorraine No?

Pete I don't . . .

Lorraine They're all on their way home in New York City. All the heavy-legged girls with their empty lunch-boxes and their pockets full of Twinkies.

Pete It's seven p.m. in New York City.

Lorraine In New York City, we haven't even met. In New York City, anything we do now has yet to happen.

Pete I'm in love with someone.

Lorraine Well. There you are then.

Pete My lover.

Lorraine Yes.

Pete She's an alchemist, wreaths and garlands, potions, vapours, she's making me live forever.

Lorraine *puts in earphones. Closes her eyes, resumes humming.*

I'm sorry. (*Louder.*) I'm sorry. (*Louder.*) I'm sorry.

Lorraine (*removing earphones*) Don't be sorry for me darling. I'm not the one living with a corpse.

Beat.

Pete Tell me about the first time.

Lorraine There was no first time.

Pete Have you ever been in love Lorraine?

Lorraine Have I ever been in love? I've been in love forever. From the first time I saw him. Square jaw in a dark bar, gold wings on his reefer. I'm a sucker for convention. He's five floors up now, licking a steamy cunt without dispersing his aftershave. I hate him.

Pete Does he love you Lorraine?

Lorraine God no. I'm a tart.

Pause.

Pete I love you.

Lorraine Gee thanks.

Pause.

Pete When I die.

Lorraine When you die?

Pete I want to be packaged. A neat ecclesiastical box full of ash and passed around my family and blessed with their accusations. 'What was that little bastard leaning over a balcony for, with all that we did to please him. What right had he to rot on us, with all that we did to cure him. The thoughtless little . . .'

Lorraine The first time . . .

Pete The first time?

Lorraine I was sitting on a rock. Saturday in May. I was ten, maybe eleven, and Dana . . . There was a boy in my brother's class, they called Dana. Dana they called him, because he could sing 'All Kinds of Everything', with the gut twisting innocence of a wee Derry virgin. And it broke your fucking heart.

Sings a couple of lines.

And then he got older, his voice broke, his lips got flaccid, his breath smelt, rivers of pus ran down his neck. And still they called him Dana. Dana. So – I'm sitting on my rock, and along comes Dana, sores weeping. And in his hand is his cock, substantial, but soft. I had been thinking what beautiful things feet were. He pointed it at me. The lumpy cock. And pissed. Sharp horse piss. Scorch. He said 'you're pregnant now'. Belgium won that night, great dresses.

Pete I'm sorry.

Lorraine What are you sorry for?

Lorraine *picks up headphones and resumes humming.*

Pete *is silent then weeps.*

Scene Seven

A hotel room. **Lorraine** *and* **Colin** *are on the bed still half dressed humping clumsily. Muffled noises come through the wall of a much more dynamic sex session.*

Colin *sighs and stops. He moves away from* **Lorraine**.

Colin Fuck. Sorry. I can't.

Lorraine *looks at him, unmoved. He stares at the floor.*

Bad idea. Really bad idea.

Lorraine *realises the sex is over. She sits up.*

I'm sorry . . . I mean, I just thought a drink and maybe . . . I'm sorry.

Lorraine What happened to 'old times' sake' then?

Colin *tries to gauge how annoyed she is. It's difficult.*

Colin I thought it might be . . .

Lorraine A trip down memory lane?

Colin Your eyes. In the bar. Downstairs. Your eyes were red. I thought you'd been crying. I thought/

Lorraine Chlorine.

Colin Eh?

Lorraine I'd been swimming.

Colin Oh. Right.

A beat.

Lorraine Don't do that you prick. I've had a bellyful of your pity. I can't stomach any more.

Colin I was only . . .

Lorraine Honest to God. It was like shagging Mother Theresa sometimes.

Colin *gives up trying to explain. The noises from next door continue.*

Colin You've not changed much, have you.

Lorraine That doesn't sound like a compliment.

Pause. **Lorraine** *goes to the mini-bar. It is empty. She kicks it.*

Fucking mini-bars. Useless.

Colin Try room service.

Lorraine No need.

She rakes in her bag and produces an airline sized bottle of wine. She opens it and drinks straight from the bottle.

Colin I'm happy, you know. With Helen. We're very happy.

Lorraine Good.

Colin She's what I need. A bit of stability.

Lorraine I'm sure she's got her feet firmly on the ground.

Colin I just couldn't get her out of my head.

Lorraine Look is this supposed to make me feel better?

A beat.

Colin Are you happy?

Lorraine Colin, fuck off.

She leans against the wall and drinks. He watches her. Through the wall the noises continue. **Lorraine** *is listening.* **Colin** *notices her distant expression.*

Colin I still think about you.

Lorraine*'s dream is disturbed. She looks at him doubtfully.*

When we won the Eurovision Song Contest again. That woman . . .

Lorraine Katrina and the Waves.

Colin I thought, I bet Lorraine's watching this. First time since Brotherhood of Man wasn't it?

Lorraine Bucks Fizz.

Colin I thought of you anyway.

Lorraine *says nothing. Drinks some more.*

Remember what you used to say?

A beat.

Never shag anyone who can't remember Abba?

Pause. **Lorraine** *is lost in thought again. Still drinking at the wall, listening to the sounds from next door.* **Colin** *watches her. He becomes increasingly uncomfortable.*

Lorraine?

She looks at him. The noise from next door continues to build up.

Jesus. These walls must be paper thin.

Lorraine Maybe they're just being loud. They usually are.

Colin Who are they?

Lorraine She's the bleach-blonde with the thick ankles you were staring at in the bar.

Colin What about him?

A beat.

Lorraine He's the one I was thinking about while you were fucking me.

A pause. **Colin***'s not sure how to deal with this.*

In fact, he's the one I always thought about while you were fucking me.

Colin *absorbs this.*

Colin It's that pilot guy, isn't it?

Lorraine It's the guy who's supposed to stop and tell her that he can't go on 'cos he can't get me out of his mind.

The noise continues.

But he never does.

She is becoming upset.

Colin Why did you want to see me, Lorraine? Why tonight? After all/

Lorraine I wanted to remember what it was like. What it was like to be loved.

Colin Even by me.

Lorraine Even by you.

Colin And?

Lorraine And I couldn't

A beat.

Colin I think I'd better go home.

He goes to the door.

Lorraine?

Lorraine *does not respond.* **Colin** *leaves.* **Lorraine** *is against the wall. She listens to the sound crescendo next door. Tears well. She faces the wall and presses herself against it. Not sexually but gently caressing.*

She starts to cry. She pounds softly at the plasterboard with her fists. Forlorn. The sex is obviously approaching climax.

Lorraine*'s beating on the wall becomes rhythmic. As the couple next door come noisily, she starts to sing – faltering, broken-voiced, to herself a melancholic 60s hit such as Sandie Shaw's 'Like a Puppet on a String'.*

The climax next door subsides.

Lorraine *continues singing.*

The noise next door quietens into low moans.

Lorraine *continues singing.*

The sound of post-coital laughter through the wall.

Lorraine *continues singing.*

Lorraine *stops singing. Gradually her fists stop beating and open out until her hands are pressed hard against the wall. As is her face and the rest of her body. As if the plaster could open up and swallow her.*

Scene Eight

Dark interior. **Helen**, *barely visible, stands at the window. Rumpled bed – coat/clothing on the bed vaguely represents a person. Enter* **Colin**. *quietly. Places shoes next to the bed, lies down.*

Colin (*whispered*) Helen . . . Helen . . .

Helen (*behind him*) What?

Colin (*turns*) Jesus. Fuck. Where . . . You're . . . Hello.

Helen Hello.

Pause.

Colin I'm sorry.

Helen For what?

Beat.

Colin It's late.

Helen Right.

Helen *lies down.*

Colin Helen?

Helen My hair. You're leaning on my hair.

Colin Sorry. Helen . . . ?

Helen What time is it?

Colin I . . .

Helen Someone phoned for you today. You're freezing.

Colin . . . Cold. Who?

Helen I dunno.

Colin What did they say?

Helen Nothing.

Colin Man or woman?

Helen Man.

Colin What did he want?

Helen He didn't say. You.

Colin Who was he?

Helen I don't know.

Beat.

Colin Sorry.

Helen I'm not a mind reader.

Colin No.

Pause.

Helen Move a bit, can you just . . .

Colin Move a bit, yeah. Helen . . .

Helen God I'm so fucking tired, why am I always so fucking tired.

Colin I dunno, everyone is tired, the . . .

Helen . . . Whole fucking world is tired. I know.

Colin Kiss me.

Beat.

Helen . . .

Helen They found a woman today.

Colin Who did?

Helen In the river. Bloated.

Colin Who?

Helen Her fingertips had exploded.

Colin Jesus. Who was . . . ?

Helen You're so cold.

Colin Helen?

Helen I don't know.

Beat.

I don't know who anyone is. They're just people. People on the phone, people in the river. Dead people. People with plastic gloves, fingerless people . . . there's so many of them, it doesn't really matter who they are.

Colin No. Do you want some . . . ?

Helen Touch me.

Colin Helen . . .

Helen You feel so cold.

Colin Helen . . .

Helen (*snaps*) Alright then don't.

Colin Helen it's just . . . I love you.

Helen Do it. Don't talk to me, just do it.

Colin I can't.

Helen Do it!

Colin I love you. I have always loved you.

Pause.

Helen The first time . . .

Colin With me?

Helen No. The first time ever. I went to him in his room, he was sleeping with elastic around his skull. I knew it was something very private.

Colin You've told me.

Helen He was so young. And he was so beautiful.

Colin You were young.

Helen It felt so simple. It felt biblical. That afternoon we lay in an open-topped van on Coca Cola crates. Once we lay under a pylon.

Colin Hold me.

Helen I don't want to hold you.

Pause.

Colin *moves away.*

Colin You're just tired.

Helen I'm not tired.

Colin You just said . . .

Helen It doesn't matter what I just said.

Colin Don't push me Helen.

Helen Don't push me Helen. Why can't you fuck me?

Colin I don't want to fuck you. I want to hold you. I love you.

Helen Stop! Stop saying 'I love you'. I love you. I love you. I love you. I love you. I love you eat. I love you drink. I love you shit. I love you old, empty, blue-veined, fish-eaten, maggot-filled, corpse, love you.

Colin Go to bed.

Pause.

Helen You'd better find someone Colin. Find them and fuck them.

Colin What are you talking about?

Beat.

Helen It was Lorraine.

Colin What?

Helen On the phone. Lorraine was the person who rang today.

Beat.

Colin What did she . . . ?

Helen . . . Want? She was selling life insurance I think, or maybe it was curtain lining. How is she?

Colin I didn't plan . . .

Helen Do you really think I give a damn?

Colin She was distressed . . . some . . .

Helen Colin, I know about your puerile leaps over the orchard wall. It's not that, it's never been that . . .

Colin I swear, I didn't . . .

Helen It's your shivering homecomings for a cup of familiar skin and sympathy. Your moist satisfaction that I am still the fairest.

Colin Stop this Helen.

Helen I am so exhausted by you. So . . . so weary of you.

Colin (*quietly*) Who is he Helen? Hmmm? Who? (*Rising.*) Who is he Helen. Who fucking is he?

Helen It doesn't matter, it never matters.

Colin *walks to* **Helen** *and strikes her forcibly.*

Colin Fuck you. Fuck you. I can, I fucking own you . . .

He attempts to rape her.

Fuck . . . weary. Fuck, see you . . . I . . . you forget . . . you forget. I have loved you, have held . . . have drowned in canals for you . . . have run across tarmacs for you . . . have smashed plates . . . windows for you. Have wept and howled for you.

Breaks down.

. . . and have held your face and cherished it, I . . . you love me.

He weeps – she holds him.

Helen Colin – you're only a moment, only a moment . . . Colin . . . you never obliterated my past, never deciphered my future.

Scene Nine

Greg *and* **Helen** *in a park. They sit, apparently picnicking, but there is a tension. They both gaze at a fixed point a few dozen yards away. A long silence is finally broken.*

Greg For God's sake! How much crap can one Labrador actually contain? I think I saw his kidneys come out a minute ago.

Beat

What d'you think she must be feeding it? Bet it's vegetarian. There's a lot of that around.

Helen Stupid bitch!

Greg Helen.

The dog owner looks towards them. **Greg** *smiles warmly and nods at her. He budges* **Helen** *to do likewise but she snarls at the woman.*

Helen She should be locked up. Children can go blind. It's disgusting.

Greg My mum used to tell me that. They'll lock you up. You'll go blind. It's disgusting.

Helen I didn't know you had a dog.

Greg *laughs.*

Don't laugh at me.

Greg I'm not.

Helen What's so funny then?

Greg It's what she said when she caught me . . . you know . . .

Helen What?

Greg Beating the meat. Doing the five-fingered shuffle. Shaking hands with/

Helen Wanking?

Greg Yeah.

Helen Oh.

Pause.

Greg I think they're going. The Labrador must be empty.

Helen Finally.

Greg *sees something else.*

Greg Shit!

Helen Fucking joggers now!

Helen *sighs with exasperation. They watch the joggers go past and then glance about them to check the coast is clear. It is. They look at each other.*

A beat.

In a second, **Helen** *is sitting across* **Greg**'*s lap, facing him.* **Greg** *fumbles with his flies. She lowers herself on to him with a groan of satisfaction.*

I hate having to wait.

Greg Anticipation is half the fun.

They kiss as **Helen** *begins to ride him forcefully.*

Helen Fuck the anticipation.

Greg *laughs then groans with pleasure as she grinds against him.*

Helen I could stay like this all day.

Greg I'm not sure I could manage that.

Helen Too much anticipation.

Greg *laughs.*

Greg You're mad.

Helen Maybe I am.

A beat. **Greg** *glances at his watch again.* **Helen** *sees and sighs.*

Greg I've got to go down to the south coast this afternoon. I don't want to miss it.

Helen Do you want to miss me?

Greg I've got to go.

Helen Stay.

Greg I can't.

A beat.

How was your week? Anything exciting?

Helen Colin hit me.

Pause.

I said, Colin/

Greg I heard.

He shrugs, not knowing what to say.

I'm sorry.

Pause.

Helen Shall we talk about the weather then?

Greg It's a beautiful day. Beautiful day. Beautiful girl.

He kisses her. She is not won over.

Helen Imagine if it was always like this.

Greg You'd get bored.

Helen Never.

Greg Everything gets boring eventually.

Helen It doesn't have to.

Greg It does. It's inevitable. Like toasters.

Helen Toasters?

Greg Built-in obsolescence. They break. You get a new one. Inevitable.

Helen I can't believe you're talking about toasters.

Greg Kettles then. They're the same.

Helen I don't want to talk about household fucking appliances.

A beat.

Greg I was only saying . . . obsolescence.

Pause.

Helen What if they don't break down? What if the toaster never breaks, it never needs fixing. Your theory falls apart.

Greg Toasters always break. It's a law of nature. It's part of the essence of toasterness.

Helen But if they don't. If they're well made. If they're built to last.

Greg They're not though. If they were, you couldn't afford them. It'd be forks in front of the fire again.

Helen But if they were?

A beat.

Greg I thought you didn't want to talk about household appliances.

Pause. **Greg** *checks the time again.* **Helen** *grabs his wrist.*

What?

Helen Let me see.

She takes off his watch.

Greg What are you doing?

Helen I'm trying to work out how it exerts its amazing power.

Greg It's just a watch.

A beat.

Come on. Give it back.

She doesn't.

Helen I've never seen you without it. You wear it all the time, don't you?

Greg Everyone wears a watch.

Helen *displays her naked wrist.*

Yeah. Well that's why you're always late, isn't it.

Helen You wouldn't know if I was always late if you weren't wearing this.

Greg No. But you'd still be late.

Helen You wouldn't know when it was time to go either.

Greg But I'd still have to go.

A beat.

Helen Were you like this when you were young?

Greg Younger.

Helen When you were a kid?

Greg I got a Timex for my tenth birthday. I've worn a watch ever since. Alright? It's not unusual.

Helen Ten? You've been like this since you were ten?

Greg I'm aware of time. That's all. Most people are. Even you.

Helen Not at ten.

Greg Twelve then? Fifteen? How can you go on your first date without knowing what time to meet?

Helen Dates and times. Times and dates.

Greg Can I have it back please? I'm going to have to go.

Helen When I was twelve I didn't have a watch. My time ticked by slower. I spent it all imagining what it would be like when I was grown up. Did you do that?

Greg Yeah. Hover-cars and living on the moon. The water . . .

Helen I mean, what *you* would be like. What you would be doing. What you would have done. Did you think about that?

Greg Of course.

Helen And now. D'you ever think now about what you're actually like, what you are doing. What you have done? D'you do that and wonder what went wrong?

Greg I wanted to be an astronaut.

Helen I wanted to be happy.

Beat.

Here.

She gives him the watch. He checks the time. She changed it.

Greg Helen!

Helen It's only quarter past, now. We've got ages. We haven't even started yet.

Greg That's stupid.

Helen What time is it, then?

Greg I don't know, do I.

Helen So let's make it quarter past.

Greg You can't do that.

Helen I can. I did.

Pause. **Greg** *tries to reset his watch.*

Were you disappointed when you realised you'd never be an astronaut? Did it hurt?

Greg No. I'd grown out of it anyway.

Helen Grown out of it? Your burning ambition?

Greg It was just a phase.

Helen A phase?

Greg It passed. Everything passes.

Helen It doesn't have to.

Greg It does. Helen . . .

Helen No. Listen. If you really want something . . .

Greg It doesn't matter.

Helen If you really believe . . .

Greg Time doesn't care what you believe. It just goes on. And everything is temporary. All of us. All of this.

Pause.

Helen Us? This?

Greg I didn't mean . . .

Pause.

Helen you know . . . we both know the situation, don't we. I really have to go.

Helen The situation?

He kisses her and gets ready to leave.

Greg Temporary doesn't mean brief.

Helen How can you . . .

Greg What?

Helen Don't you . . . Don't you want to believe that some things . . . One thing . . . That one single thing might . . . endure . . . Don't you want that? Don't you need that?

Greg It's a nice idea . . .

Helen But . . . ?

Greg What we want doesn't matter. Desire doesn't alter the facts.

Helen What if desire is the fact? What if desire is the only fact that matters? What if physics was based on passion? And chemistry was about love? What if the world turned on a whim and . . . and gravity came from the heart? What if this was that place? Us. Here. Now. What if this was the world and we could live there? What if?

A beat.

Would you stay?

Greg I have to go.

Helen Stay.

A beat.

Greg I can't.

Scene Ten

An interview room. **Greg** *holds two cans of different cola – one in each hand.*

Annie So, Greg. Spring, summer, autumn or winter?

Greg I really don't know. Anne.

Annie Annie. Try washing it around, Greg. Washing it around your mouth before you swallow. Some people find that helps.

Greg If you like.

He washes the cola around his mouth.

Annie Well?

Beat.

Don't think about it Greg. Taste it and then just say. The season this cola evokes for me is . . . blah, blah, blah. Yes?

Greg I'm going to go.

Annie No. Please.

Greg This is stupid. I don't want to do this. I haven't got the time.

Annie Please. This is important for me. I'm paid for each completed questionnaire. And I need more men. For my profile. I've done plenty of women and now I need older m – men in your demographic constituency. I can't afford to waste time. I have to do four of these to make two pounds an hour. I can't afford to waste ten minutes. So. Spring, summer, autumn, winter?

Greg I really don't know.

Annie Anything, say anything.

Greg Anything.

Annie Please.

Greg Spring.

Annie Thank you.

Greg I see you're not wearing a watch.

Annie Next question.

Greg Someone who cares about the time should own a watch. I've got several.

Annie If this cola was a female movie star . . . Clock. I keep an eye on that clock . . . if this cola was a female movie star I'd say this cola was . . . ?

Greg Someone should buy you a watch. Winona Ryder.

Annie Really? That's very interesting Greg. Because it's . . . give me some words.

Greg Pert . . . twinkly . . . welcoming. I would have thought your parents would have bought you a watch.

Annie I don't see my parents. Next box.

Greg That's very sad. Or maybe your boyfriend.

Annie The other cola. Same question.

Greg Female movie star?

Annie Female movie star.

Greg Sharon Stone.

Annie Very interesting Greg, because . . .

Greg It has no undies on.

Annie Yes?

Greg Am I embarrassing you Anne? Yes, This cola is brazen. This cola is not wearing any panties.

Annie Thank you.

Greg Is this the kind of thing that you want?

Annie I want whatever you've got to say Greg. Because it's not about me. It's not about what I want. I'm neutral.

Greg Do you have a boyfriend? I think your boyfriend should buy you a watch. Surely you weren't christened Annie?

Annie I can't get involved on any personal level.

Greg A lot of young women today seem very lonely. Mobile phone stuck on the head like you'd need a surgeon to remove it. And they're talking away twenty-four hours a day. 'I'm lonely, I'm lonely'.

Annie If you had to choose, Greg. A night with Winona Ryder or a night with Sharon Stone? Which would you choose?

Greg I don't think that's likely to happen.

Annie Yes. But hypothetically.

Greg Look, if you want to know which taste of cola I prefer, then just ask me. Let's not do all this stuff. Let's just be honest with each other Anne. Which name were you christened with?

Annie Please. This is how they do it in the questionnaire. This is the way they like to do it. So if you could just . . . Which one would you choose to sleep with?

Greg I wouldn't choose either of them.

Annie But if you had to pick one.

Greg I wouldn't. Do you know who I fancy Anne? Do you know what stirs my sleeping beast? Do you?

Annie Annie is on my birth certificate. That's my real name.

Greg I don't fantasise about women I'll never meet. Who needs to when around you there are so many women? Lonely women who just want somebody to reach out to them.

Annie Are you answering my question?

Greg Do you know Anne – I think I probably am. Who needs to choose Sharon or Winona, pert or no knickers, when every day you find yourself sitting opposite a real woman. A real, lonely woman.

Annie Shall I put Sharon Stone? My name's Annie.

Greg And so few men see it. So few understand that all these women are looking for is – what? Company? Release?

Annie I'll put Sharon Stone.

Greg Do you know what I'm saying Annie? I think that's why women cling on to me.

Greg *takes off his watch.*

Here.

Annie What?

Greg I want you to have this.

Annie I can't

Greg Someone's got to look after you. Parents who've spurned you.

Annie It's not like that.

Greg Boyfriend who can't spare a penny from his Giro.

Annie Please. I can't get personally involved.

Greg Alright then. If that's what you want.

Annie Sorry.

Greg If that's what's important to you.

Annie We're almost there, OK?

Greg Alright.

Annie Now. If one of those colas tastes of the future, which of these colas is it?

Greg *tastes the two colas.*

Greg This one . . .

Annie Because the future is . . .

Greg Empty. Bleak. It rots your teeth.

Annie The future rots your teeth?

Greg That's not what you wanted to hear.

Annie No, no.

Greg You want to hear anything I've got to say.

Annie Yes. (*Writes.*) The future rots your teeth.

Greg You're very contained aren't you Annie? Lots of people develop that as a way of getting by. I think sometimes I shouldn't lay myself open as much as I do. Lay yourself open and you get hurt.

Annie And finally, would you describe your relationship with each of these colas as a one night stand, an affair, a marriage or a reunion?

Greg What?

Annie I know. I don't make this up. I just ask the questions. Your relationship to these colas is . . .

Greg No relationship.

Annie Please. If you pick one.

Greg You've taught me something today Annie. And I'm grateful for that. You've taught me not to lay myself open.

Annie Say something. It's the last question. My relationship to these colas is . . .

Greg No. I'm celibate. From now on I'm a monk with a vasectomy, and no libido.

Annie I don't have a box for that.

Greg Oh well. That's where I stand.

Annie What am I going to do? There's no box.

Scene Eleven

A bedsit. **Ryan** *and* **Annie** *enter.*

Ryan But did you enjoy it? Really? I thought you might get a bit bored. It's an old film and a lot of people/

Annie It was brilliant. I loved it.

Ryan Yeah? Honestly? You're not just/

Annie Honestly.

A beat. **Ryan** *believes her. He relaxes a bit.*

Ryan You can get it on video but it's much better on a big screen.

Annie The bit where she goes looking for Cat . . .

Ryan I know.

Annie And she was so beautiful.

Ryan Yeah. She really was.

A beat.

I'm glad you liked it. I hoped you would.

Annie I loved it.

Pause. **Ryan** *remembers something. He produces a bottle from under the bed.*

Champagne? Are we celebrating something?

Ryan No . . . I just . . . I though it would be nice. Y'know. I didn't mean.

Annie It's alright.

Ryan If you'd rather not, I could/

Annie Ryan, I'd love some.

Ryan Great.

Ryan *starts to open it.*

Annie You should stick it in the fridge for a while first. Chill it.

Ryan D'you think? I wouldn't know. I don't normally . . .

Annie Yeah.

Ryan How about the window-ledge? If I put it in the fridge someone'll nick it.

He puts it out on the window-ledge. **Annie** *looks through his CDs.*

I can't play anything. The stereo's broken.

Annie Oh.

Ryan But look. We can dance.

Annie With no music?

Ryan Easy. Come here.

They stand facing each other.

Now think of a good tune to dance to.

Annie I can't think.

Ryan Anything then.

Annie The song in the film.

Ryan 'Moon River'. Right. Good. Now remember it. Play it in your head.

Annie *laughs.*

Go on.

Annie Alright.

Pause.

Ryan Is it playing?

Annie *nods.*

Ryan *takes her hand in one of his, the other hand at her waist. She puts her other hand on his shoulder. They stay face to face.* **Ryan** *smiles as* **Annie** *begins to sway. He feels the gentle rhythm and they start to dance, tentatively.* **Annie** *relaxes and smiles at him. They dance a little closer – cheek to cheek. Eventually they sway to a stop and stay close for a moment before moving apart a little.*

Annie I like that song.

Ryan You played it very well.

Annie I've never danced like that before.

Ryan Me neither.

Pause.

Your hands are cold.

He leads her over and they sit on the floor in front of the fire/heater. She warms her hands and raises them to her cheeks and then ears. He watches her, smiling. She notices.

Annie What?

Ryan You reminded me of something.

A beat.

A rhyme. My gran taught my sister and me when we were little. It's daft.

Annie No. Say it.

Ryan *hesitates then recites slowly, making an effort to remember, looking at* **Annie**.

Ryan (*hands over his ears*) May my ears be deaf before they hear you lie.

(*Hands over his eyes.*) May my eyes go blind before you lose your charms.

(*Fingers at his lips.*) May my lips be dumb before they speak goodbye.

(*Hand on heart.*) May my heart stand still before you leave my arms.

Annie That's lovely.

She tries to recite it back, repeating the gestures. **Ryan** *helps her when she falters.*

May my ears be deaf before they hear you lie. May my eyes go blind . . .

Ryan Before you lose your charms.

Annie May my lips be dumb before they speak goodbye. May my heart . . .

Ryan Stand still.

Annie Before you leave my arms.

A pause. **Ryan** *takes one of* **Annie**'*s hands and holds it to his ear. He reaches out with his other hand to cover her ear – she covers this with her own hand. A beat. They recite the words slowly in their heads.* **Ryan** *moves* **Annie**'*s hand across his eyes.* **Annie** *does likewise with his.*

Pause. He moves her hand to his lips. She moves his to hers. A pause. He moves her hand to his heart. She moves his to hers. A long pause. He moves her hand back to his lips and kisses it. She doesn't move. He carries on kissing until she begins to stroke his face. He reaches across and does likewise. Slowly he leans in towards her. She moves her head to meet him. They kiss.

Ryan I've wanted to kiss you for so long. I've wondered what it would be like. I thought I might never get the chance.

Annie Why?

Ryan I noticed you. You were just . . . just different.

Annie Different?

Ryan Special. I thought you seemed special.

Annie I'm not special.

Ryan You are.

Annie You think?

Ryan Yeah. That's what I liked about you . . . like . . . That's what I like.

Annie I don't know what to say.

A pause.

Ryan Say you'll stay. Here. Tonight.

Annie *considers.*

Annie I think that'd be nice.

Ryan *smiles. They kiss again.*

Ryan You're really beautiful.

Annie Bet you say that to all the girls.

Ryan No.

Annie I was only kidding.

Ryan I don't do this . . . I mean I've never . . . I've never done this before . . .

A pause.

I wanted it to be special. With someone special. That's why . . .

Annie I didn't realise.

Ryan I shouldn't have said anything. I always talk too much.

Annie Ryan . . .

Ryan Do you want to go now?

Annie No. I just think . . .

Ryan If you want to wait . . .

Annie Ryan.

Ryan You are beautiful though. I mean it.

Annie You don't really know me.

Ryan I do. I know you're funny and kind and gentle . . .

Annie But . . .

Ryan And I know that I'd rather be with you. Here. Now. Than anywhere else. With anyone else.

A beat.

Annie Ryan. You want this to be special/

Ryan It is.

Annie But . . .

Ryan *puts his hand to her lips.*

Ryan Here. Now. It is. Isn't it?

Annie *shakes her head.* **Ryan** *smiles and takes his hand away.* **Anne** *looks at him. Strokes his face.*

Annie Can we put the light out?

A beat. Blackout.

Scene Twelve

Night – a garage, lit only by a corporate moon. **Ryan** *is sitting behind a till, reading, he occasionally swigs from a can of cola. He is bored and pissed off, as* **Sarah** *approaches.*

There is an imaginary sheet of Perspex between **Ryan** *and* **Sarah**. **Sarah** *goes to open the door. It's locked. She taps on the glass.* **Ryan** *looks up from his magazine, gestures to her to come over to the booth.*

Sarah *walks over. She talks through what sounds like a Tannoy, operated by push-button, pressed by* **Ryan**.

Ryan It's locked.

Sarah Twenty Marlboro Lights.

Ryan *does not speak, reaches for a packet of cigarettes and places them on the counter.* **Sarah** *pays.*

Thirty-eight per cent of the female sector between 23 and 35 express a preference for Marlboro Lights based on a desire to give up.

Sarah *sees that he is drinking the can of cola.*

I notice you're drinking . . .

Ryan Huh?

Sarah Cola. You're drinking *the* cola.

Ryan Yeah . . . Do you want petrol?

Sarah No thank you.

Ryan *flicks off the button and carries on reading.* **Sarah** *stands in the courtyard contemplating* **Ryan**. *She goes to speak again.*

Ryan (*pressing the button*) Yes.

Sarah I will have something . . . I'll have some . . . I'll have a can of that drink . . .

Ryan *looks at her pissed off and gets up to get her a can of the drink. He slides it under the glass.* **Sarah** *slides the money back under the glass.*

He rings up his till. He gives her change.

. . . Thank you . . . (*Reading his button badge.*) What's your name?

Ryan Geronimo.

Sarah I bet.

Ryan *goes back to his reading.* **Sarah** *waits, opens her drink, drinks, contemplates it. Tapping on the window.* **Ryan** *reluctantly presses the button.*

Ryan The ladies' are round the back. I can give you a key.

Sarah Sorry?

Ryan If you've got a punter.

Sarah Sorry?

Ryan They've just been in to clean them so don't make a mess.

Sarah Listen you little –

Ryan *flicks the switch off.* **Sarah** *stops mid sentence.* **Ryan** *returns to his reading. Pause. She gestures to him again.*

Ryan I'll call security.

Sarah Tell me your name?

Ryan It initiates an alarm if you stay on the forecourt too long.

Sarah Please . . .

Ryan It's my security PIN. We're not allowed to give our real names.

Sarah (*pointing*) *That* cola –

Ryan *looks at her, then looks at the can, bemused.*

You like the taste of *that* cola.

Ryan I was thirsty.

Sarah So you went to the shelf and you –

Sarah *takes out a cigarette, goes to light it.*

Ryan You can't . . .

Sarah *stops herself and puts it away.*

I haven't got any money in here. It's externally operated. They change it every thirty minutes.

Sarah You're 'a'. Spice. Knew what you wanted – *that* cola – what you really, really wanted and you got it.

Ryan It was by the till.

Sarah It was by the till and –

Ryan Can I get you something else?

Sarah And?

Ryan What?

Sarah It was by the till and . . . Why? What went through your mind? Before you bent down? Rows and rows of other brands, other tastes but something made you pick this one up. It was by the till, on that bottom shelf, not an easy reach, but if you're a Spice you know what you want what you really, really want and –

Sarah *waits in hopeful anticipation.* **Ryan** *looks at her. A long beat.*

Ryan That end, they don't pick it up on the camera.

Sarah *looks at him. The bubble bursts.*

Sarah (*almost to herself*) Geronimo!

Pause.

Ryan I've got a phone . . .

Sarah You're reading?

Ryan . . . in case of accidents or emergencies . . .

Sarah I want to see.

Ryan *looks at her. Considers.*

Ryan It's nothing.

Sarah Show me.

Pause. **Ryan** *holds up the book to the glass – a comic.*

Rom the Space Knight . . . (**Sarah** *almost laughs to herself.*) What does he do then?

Ryan He's a Space Knight . . .

Sarah Really.

Ryan Yeah . . .

A beat.

Sarah So he's a Space Knight . . .

Ryan Not always. (*A beat.*) He worked on a farm with . . . Judy . . .

Sarah His beautiful wife . . . ?

Ryan Yeah . . .

Sarah In gingham.

Ryan Is that the checked stuff?

Sarah *does not even bother to answer.*

You're blocking the forecourt.

Sarah *does not answer. A long pause.*

Sarah Is he good to his wife?

A beat.

Ryan Um . . . she's not in it anymore but . . . He takes her out to dinner and ploughs the field and stuff. She puts things in jars. They've got a kid and then . . .

Sarah How touching.

Ryan I haven't read it in a long time . . . I don't anymore . . . Only . . . today . . . Something made me – just – flick through it again. I don't . . .

Sarah Lighten up, Space Knight.

Ryan Please.

Sarah Let me in.

Ryan Lock doesn't un-click 'til the next shift.

Sarah Have you got someone? A girlfriend.

Ryan *flicks off the button. He does not answer.* **Sarah** *taps on the glass.* **Ryan** *flicks the button back on.*

Ryan I don't know.

Sarah Tell me the rest of the story.

Pause.

Tell me . . . When did he get his calling, then?

Pause. **Ryan** *flicks the switch on.*

Ryan Um. One day. Standing in a field looking over the corn. There's a dog yapping and a little boy chasing his tail and Judy's in all the checked stuff and hanging out the washing and suddenly . . . blinding flash of light and . . .

Ryan *flicks up the volume.*

Rom. We have been sent the forces of good and evil. The time has come. You have been chosen to join our team of warrior fighters, turn your heart to steel and become the lone Space Knight, travelling the universe, and defeating the masters of darkness.

Ryan *sits back, suddenly self conscious.*

Sarah So he turns his heart to steel and gets into the spaceship and blasts off saving the world. (*A beat.*) And sometimes when he smells an expensive perfume or is touched by something familiar he thinks of . . . What's her name?

Ryan Judy.

Sarah And a tear comes to his eye. All alone. On the moon one in three . . . Poor fucking Judy.

Ryan He doesn't give a fuck about Judy. He just doesn't give a fuck . . . Space Knights don't need her . . . They fight, and they save lives and they fuck beautiful aliens with green tits and space wenches in silver heels and they're just brilliant . . . They're just . . . brilliant.

Sarah How old are you?

Ryan Nineteen . . .

Sarah Geronimo, when I was nineteen I wanted to be held very tender, very close, and I wanted someone to love me and I'd love them and they'd care about me and laugh with me and live with me and die with me. They'd stroke my hair, and touch me and hold me in their arms and tell me they were my biggest fan and I'd *want* them and they'd *want* me and they wouldn't sleep around. They'd just lie with me, stay still, stay with me, love just me . . . me . . . Do you think that's possible?

Ryan *leans forward, as if almost to kiss her, thinking on the moment.*

Ryan You're weird.

Ryan *leans forward and steals another can from the shelf.* **Sarah** *stands watching him.*

Sarah We're gonna light up the moon tonight.

A beat.

Ryan (*sarcastic*) Wow.

Sarah *turns and walks away.*

Lightning Source UK Ltd.
Milton Keynes UK
UKOW04f0326310315

248809UK00001B/17/P